If she only knew...

If she only knew that I
didn't get to eat supper
last night, she wouldn't
have taken the extra
cereal that Chris gave me
at breakfast. She said,
"Only one cereal for each student.
That's the rule at this school."

If she only knew...

If she only knew that I
had to watch my little
brother last night while
momma was at the park with
her friends, she wouldn't
have punished me for not
getting my homework done.

If she only knew...

If she only knew that I
like to make stuff during
science class, she would
let us make rockets like
Mrs. Bagen's class.
Instead, we read about
rockets from a book.

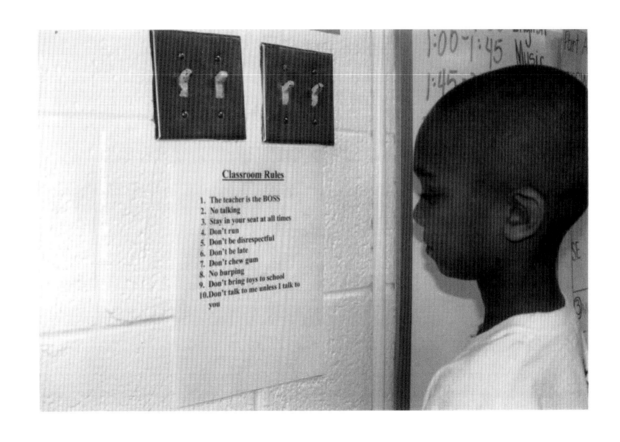

If she only knew...

If she only knew that
her rules are as long as the
lines at the city pool,
she would make a shorter
list that we could remember.

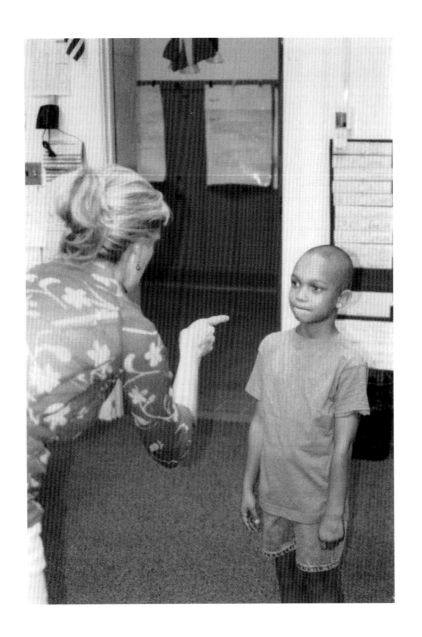

If she only knew...

If she only knew that my
daddy left me and momma
when I was two, she would
stop telling me that she's
going to call my daddy for
a conference.

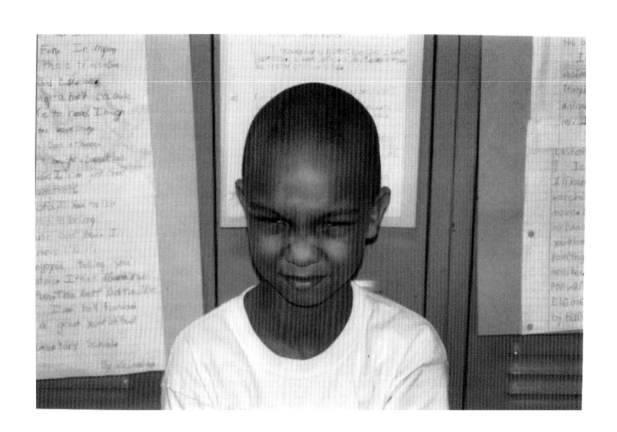

If she only knew...

If she only knew that I
get really upset when
Leonard talks about my
momma, her biggest rule
would be, "No talking about
other people's mommas."

If she only knew...

If she only knew how much
I love to draw, she would
make me the class poster
maker. Instead, she doesn't
let me because my
handwriting isn't so great.

If she only knew...

If she only knew that I
need to talk if I'm going
to learn, she wouldn't send
me to the principal's
office so much. She says
my talking is disruptive
in the classroom. She's
the only person talking.
In my opinion, that's a disruption.

If she only knew...

If she only knew that when
she gets mad and screams
at the class it scares me.
Last year, Mrs. Stewley
never raised her voice at
me. Mrs. Stewley was as
quiet as a crook after midnight.
When Mrs. Stewley talked,
kids listened.

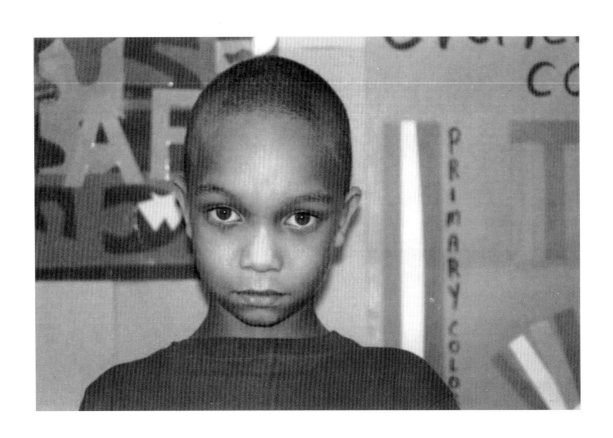

If she only knew...

If she only knew that some
of the boys are trying to
get me to join their gang,
she would help me say,
"No."

If she only knew...

If she only knew how much
I like to run, she would
have told me about last
week's track team sign-up.

If she only knew...

If she only knew how much I need
my mentor here at school,
she would let me see him more.
He thinks I'm cool.

If she only knew...

If she only knew that I
had to get my little
brother up and ready for
school this morning, she
wouldn't have fussed at me
for being a few minutes late.

**"No significant learning occurs
without a significant relationship."
-Dr. James Comer**

This book is dedicated to our children:
Mason, Amanda, Haley, and Vivian.

We would like to thank the students at
Foust Elementary School in Owensboro, Kentucky.
You have touched our lives in a very special way, and
you have changed the way we think about school.

To our readers:
May this book inspire and challenge you to discover the unique potential
in each of your students. As educators, it is our responsibility not only to teach
our students but also to nurture their souls. It is imperative that we look beyond
their eyes and into their hearts . . . remember, every child has a story.

Rocket Publishing
A Limited Liability Company

www.rocketpublishing.net